Poetry of Love

Poetry of Love

I Love You

Dr. Daniel Simon Pierre

Preface

This book is about all my personal and private expressions of love.

In my opinion, love is mental, physical, emotional, and surely spiritual. For example, the Bible tells us in John 3:16, "For God so love the world that he gave his only begotten son so that whosoever believes in him shall not perish but have everlasting life."

I was never a good talking, a playboy, or a romantic person. In fact, before meeting and courting my wife, the two longest relationships lasted only two months. But when I met and got to know my church sister - now my wife, everything changed. I opened myself to love, took chances, and acted very corny and needy, meaning myself.

I thank my wife for having loved me for 25 years now (and counting). I also thank God for showing us how to love each other despite our many differences.

I think the readers will find, know, and experience love while reading this book. My advice to the reader is to start planning for the engagement party, the wedding, and be ready to fall in love, make love, and *be in love*. Though not a guarantee, the result may vary. Yes, also remember not to be afraid, trust, and give yourself away in the arms of someone else (preferably a man and a woman, which is my core belief).

My intention is simply to keep loving, to touch every dormant love and emotional nerves, and to have the reader think of and want to fall in love, love, *and be in love*.

Lastly, I desire to connect to each of my readers on a personal, emotional, spiritual, psychological, and physical basis, and help them to be love, feel love, and stay in love as I did, do, and will.

I love my wife.

Jesus Two

Jesus is the answer of the world today,
in a world full of confusion, turmoil, wars,
and rumor of wars.
I need Jesus.

Oh, how I love Jesus!
How can you love him who you do not see
and not your neighbor who you see?
You need Jesus.

Jesus is the way, the truth, and the life.
We must show the lost the way,
tell the truth, and save lives.
We need Jesus.

Shalom

Shalom, Jerusalem,
Shalom, Israel

Peace be still.
And know that I am God
who forms the valleys
and leaves on the hills?

Sabbath Shalom, Jerusalem
Sabbath Shalom, Israel

I am the God of your ancestors,
the God of Abraham, the God of Isaac,
and the God of Jacob.
March to the temples and synagogues
to offer sacrifices of praise and worship me.

Shalom Aleichem, Jerusalem.
Shalom Aleichem, Israel.
I have delivered you
from bondage of the Egyptians.
I have delivered you
also from the Persians.
I have delivered you
again from the Philistines.
I have sent you a Savior
to deliver you from the Romans.
And I have sent you a Messiah
to deliver you from sins.

The Beauty of a Black Woman

Twin perfectly well-rounded mountain peaks
surely kindly delicious ready to be adore.

Course black hair for Tarzan
to swing from tree to tree.
Seductive eyes, clear like crystal
with perfect vision.

Flatten rounded tip cool nose,
able to detect a charlatan from far.
Ears succulent for the enabler,
sweeter than wild honey.

Tastes buds of flavor of love spread
and shadowing her delicious tongue.
Her sparkling perfectly aligns teeth
surely make the ivory tusk of African craft envious.

Spirits of My Ancestors Set Me Free

The spirits of our ancestors run deep
and warm through my veins.
Reminding me of the pain and suffering
long endured for it was not in vain.

"One day we shall surely succeed",
proclaimed Mark Twain.
Formers ancestry slaves,
now finally ruling the free world.

We are strong and resilient.
As were our ancestors' silent and profound spirits.

My Ebony

Black you are, thanks to the good God above.
Streams of thy strength flow through your veins.

Roots go deeps into the earth.
Kindly ushering the birth of our offspring.

Princesses, queens of monarchy,
only you are my perfect ebony.

A strong will and skin texture
foremost resistant to the trials, getting ready for the rapture.

Symphony of Love

Drumbeats rhythm of the season
like Beethoven's symphony of love.

Shakespeare's Broadway production of Romeo and Juliet,
south entry and exit into the portal of love.

Cadence balance to the six cords,
each note perfectly harmonized.

Do you or do you not want to know rhymes?
For the call and showers of love is soon to come.

Roots

The blood of sorrow and pain of my ancestors
cried from within,
set me free and let me go!

To what I must reach to the higher deity,
to sore high, high like the Black angels of old.

Not fallen from disgrace,
but made in his image.

Lashes torn and imbedded our skins,
from the master's bloody dirty whip
keep me tagged and labeled.

Do this, do that, thinking I would not mine,
surely, I do, surely, I must go far.

To my bellowed land far away,
yes, back home to the dawn of a new day.

Phases of Flowers

Roses are red.
Violets are blue.
I hate you,
but you hate me too.
The divorce phase.

Roses are red.
Violets are blue.
I love you,
And you love me too.
Dating phase.

Roses are red.
Violets are blue.
I do not know what I must do,
and so, do you?
Honeymoon phase.

The Most Hated Man in America

Who is this man full of pride and joy,
a tradesman and businessperson full of energy?

His only crime was to be born in opulence.
With a silver spoon in his mouth of a golden appearance

History was made when he came down
from the golden escalator inside the Trump Tower,
when he announced his historic presidential run
indeed to surely make things better for the USA.

His golden, shiny, sprayed hair,
attract and pull you in the snare.

His charisma and up-front spoken mind,
tells you like it is whether you like it or not.

It is the "New York" in him,
which flows warm like a flood.

A new wave and motto have come:
"Make America Great Again".

Senses

Eyes, big angry eyes, looking at me,
as if looking for one to see.
Seducing glare of sensuality,
privately staring at me.

Dark distant sounds in the night pierce my peace
which I thought I should not dream.
For a land far away,
that I dreamt to go all day.

Delicious aromas engage my taste buds,
to taste the sweetness of your embrace.
For it has been said,
the darker the berry, the sweeter the juice.

To feel you penetrate my core.
This immense peace forever.
Go far and far inside,
for there is even more real estate to explore.

Like a sweet aroma in the Garden of Eden,
your lovely fragrance overwhelms all my senses.
Aroma of roses, gardenias, and jasmines
forever looming from now to the end.

The Love Languages

The time we cherish together
would be forever embedded in my mind.
My heart is overwhelmed by the quality
and not the quantity of time we spent together.

I want you; I need you, and you need you.
I cannot leave without as you only can do.
You are lovely, you are specular, you are magnificent.
For only you can understand my unspoken love accent.

You are an angel sent from above,
a perfect woman with no flaws which I adore.
You are wrapped in a bundle of love
sent via express mail from above.

My mind, my body, and my soul are for you,
to serve, please, and do what you want me to do.
A foot massage, a back rub, or internal penetration
for an internal orgasm without limitation.

I want to please you.
I want to touch you.
I want to please you.
And to do what only I can do.

It Hurt (Molestation)

My angelic innocence was stolen
one dreary raining dark chilly night,
as I recall the horror and terror of what I felt
unwanted sexual advances required of me,
which I did not ask for or needed to be.

I was the prey in the domicile
for the hunter's grasp griped me from behind.
Not like a friendly familiar embrace from my beloved siblings,
but from an older man which I was unwilling.

He took the parental vow to protect and do no harm,
so why he came to my room late that night and cause me harm?
Mommy, where are you, where are you, are you sleeping?
Do you know and are you willing?

Closing your eyes to the unbearable truth,
that the man you wedded could be so untrue.
The illegal and unwanted touch
made me feel dirty and ugly,
losing my innocence far too early.

It did not happen only once from a night of drinking.
But repeated and felt its ugly hands night after night in worry.

No longer innocent, pure, or a virgin,
what would I tell my husband,
or should I tell my story from the beginning?

For the pain was, is, and will be
each night the nightmare began.
For it hurts so much and I want it to end.

The Cold (Auschwitz)

Back then, yes back, unprovoked, and unchallenged
in the cold, summer, or spring
packed like Kosher sardines to an unwanted destination.

The largest of the German Nazi concentration camps.
Over 1.1 million men, women, and children Jews were exter-
minated.
The bright star of David lit no more,
dimed, dark, in unseen horror.

Our Holocaust of accusation and extermination
started with false claims, accusations, and Kristallnacht.
Everything taken away will lose given to the predator.

But was it a secret, or all new but did not care?
They were only Gypsies and only unwanted Jews
which Hitler choose to eradicate and destroy?

He forgot his past and heritage.
His mother was a Jew, you know.

Train rides to no men land',
no boarding passes no return expected.
On the way to the gas chamber, you know.
The fastest way to see them go.

Bullets have become too expensive and take too long to kill,
the war soon ending, let us hide the burning bodies,
horrors, atrocities, and cruelty.

Poetry of Love

Six million too many gone too soon,
striped of the dignity and cultural identity
in this dreary cold dark night.

Invaded by the mighty Nazi's brutality.
Poland showed no resistance to this crisis.
Three different camps of no man-land.

Could we comprehend this disaster again?
The killing machine is on full display.
No room to grow or stay awake.
Two years of hell from 1940 -1942,
finally closed in 1945
after the liberation from the Soviet army.
1.1 million perished and died at Auschwitz.
Including one million Jews
sent to the gas chambers.
Or sentenced to forced labor
for repayment of the false accusation of
economical horror.

Sadly, the Nazi's killing machine at it's best,
as we were forced to pass the test.
Killing centers of concentration and labor camps
and the large gas chamber, smoke, cannot breathe, suffocating
and damp.

Families separated from birth breaking the bondage of lineage.
For small, medium, and large families to fit and die.

Crematoria at Birkenau,
who is left to forget our rights and say no.
Mass murder camps and mass murder ramps
only contracted and constructed for European Jews.

Afterword

Hello again, my dearest, faithful readers, and followers! Thanks to BooxAI and the great professional supporting collaborative team, I have other upcoming books and will continue to write and encourage the public until I run out of ideas.

After writing a series of poetry books (10 or 15) my goals, if the good Lord permits, are to write a cooking book (December), an exercise book (January), secular novels, and Christian motivation books in the near future, Sunday school books, sermons books, and a prayer book.

But in the meantime, please enjoy my first three submissions:

Book of Poetry (I Shall Rise)
Words from Above (Inspired)
Poetry of Love (I Love You)

Respectfully yours,

Dr. Daniel Simon Pierre
Writer / Poet
"The French Collection"